Elephant

Lion

Tiger

Bear

Rhino

Parrot

Crow

Eagle

Owl

Kingfisher

Orchid

Temple

Lilly

Rose

Lotus

Camera

Chair

Mug

Laptop

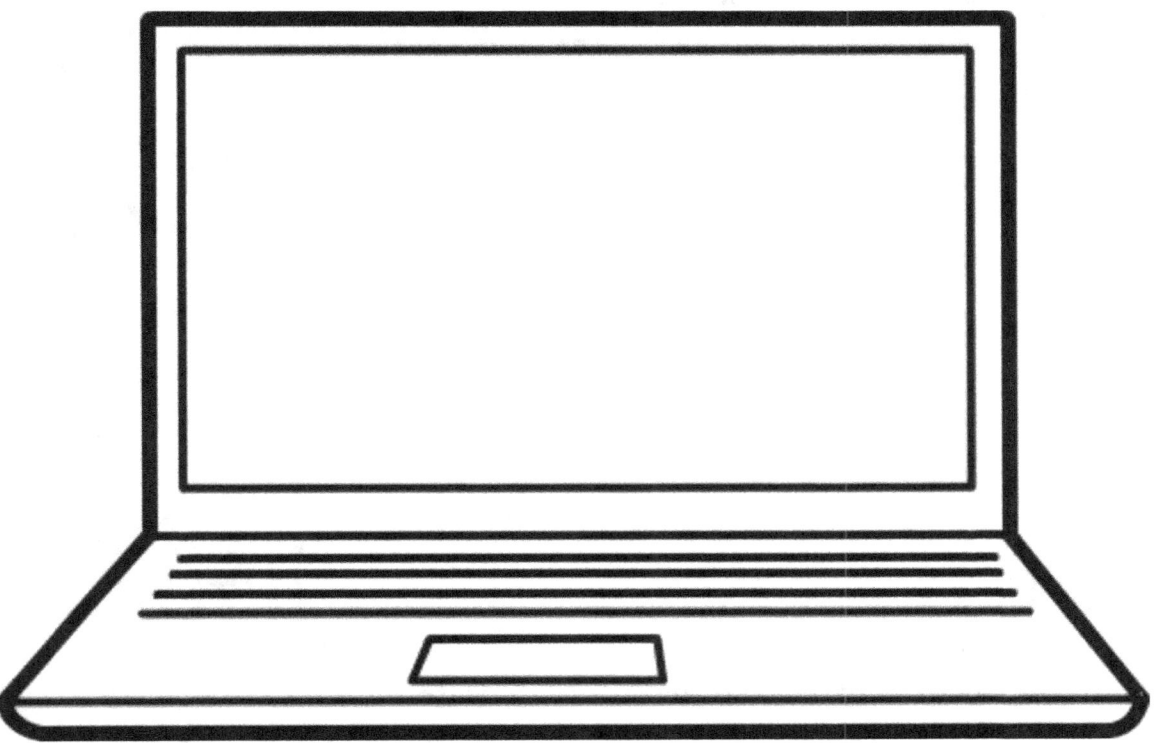

Tv

Bus

Bike

Car

Van

Rail

Eagle

Crow

Parrot

Kingfisher

Owl

Laptop

Tv

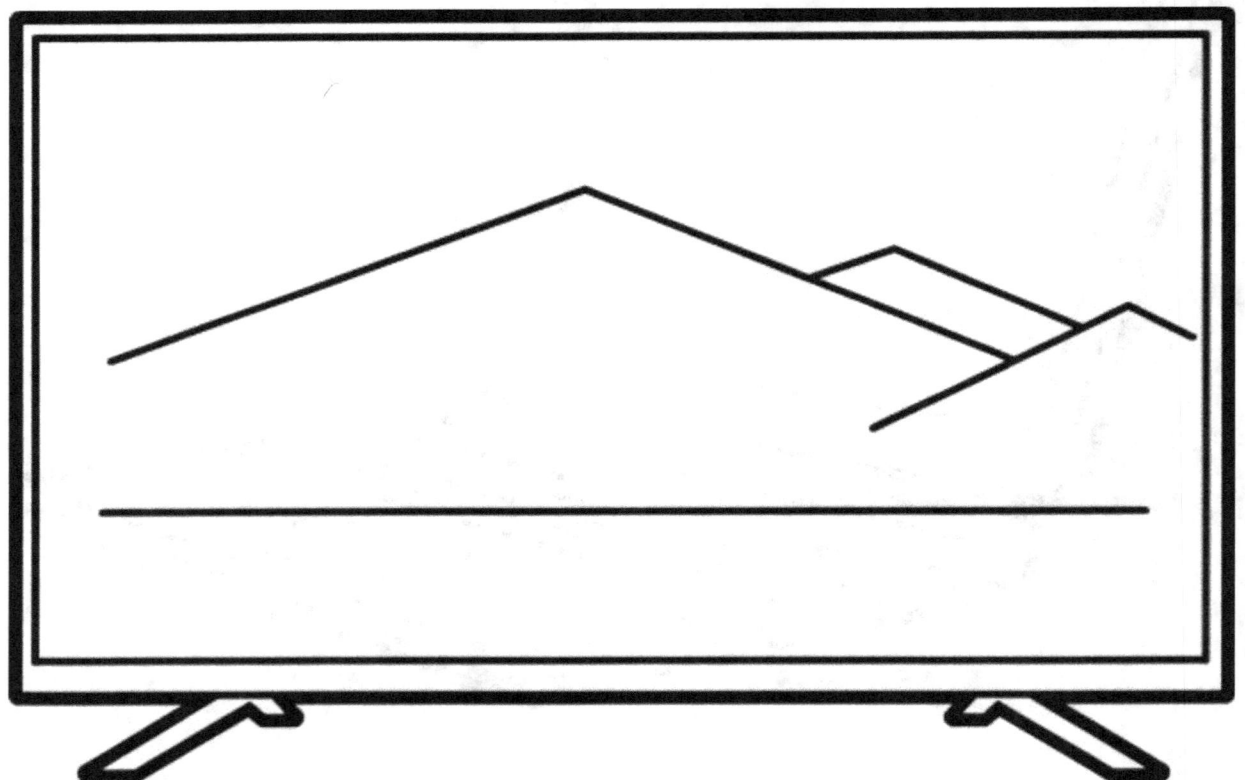

Camera

Chair

Mug

www.ingramcontent.com/pod-product-compliance
Lightning Source LLC
Chambersburg PA
CBHW081707220526
45466CB00009B/2905